The OliveOlive

Mediterranean Cookbook

45 delicious recipes from our family to yours

PAM & ROB MARSDEN

**The OliveOlive
Mediterranean Cookbook**

©2021 Rob & Pam Marsden &
Meze Publishing Limited

First edition printed in 2021 in the UK

ISBN: 978-1-910863-73-2

Written by: Rob & Pam Marsden

Edited by: Katie Fisher & Phil Turner

UK Photography by: Tim Green

Cyprus photos by:
Andrew Nicolas and Alice Vuap

Additional Photography: Julian Eales
(www.ealesphotography.co.uk),
Emily Reed
(www.emilyreedphotography.com)

Dominika Scheibinger
(www.eightysixstudios.co.uk)

Designed by: Paul Cocker

PR: Emma Toogood

Contributors: Lucy Anderson,
Suki Broad, Lizzy Capps,
Michael Johnson, Alexander McCann,
Paul Stimpson

Printed and bound in the UK by
Bell & Bain Ltd, Glasgow

Published by Meze Publishing Limited
Unit 1b, 2 Kelham Square
Kelham Riverside
Sheffield S3 8SD

Web: www.mezepublishing.co.uk

Telephone: 0114 275 7709

Email: info@mezepublishing.co.uk

ACKNOWLEDGEMENTS

We would like to thank the following people for helping to make this cookbook happen…

Firstly, to Bambos Karageorgios for producing the best extra virgin olive oil in the world and the Stefani family for making the finest halloumi cheese known to mankind.

Pam's mum and dad, Nicos and Chloe Georgiades, Uncle Takis (Uncle Ducks) and Aunt Georgia Solomonides who collectively form the Cyprus branch of OliveOlive and make things happen for us.

Friends and family who contributed with their recipes:

Anita Kearns, thank you for all your help in the kitchen

Marta Wierzbicka

Ola Maskiewicz

Costas Tsikkos

Zoiro Stefani

Georgia Solomonides

Chloe Georgiades

All the super talented chefs who provided recipes:

Maria Broadbent from Casa www.casabse.co.uk

Frank Boddy from Wild in the Pantry www.wildinthepantry.co.uk

Pascal Canevet from Maison Bleue www.maisonbleue.co.uk

Mark Frith from The Crown Inn at Broughton www.thecrowninnrestaurant.co.uk

Lindsey Kennedy from Compton & Kennedy Emporium www.comptonandkennedy.co.uk

Scott Martin from The Stove at Bourn www.thestovebourn.co.uk

Sean Melville from Bedford Lodge Hotel www.bedfordlodgehotel.co.uk

George Upshall from Nurtured and Wild www.instagram.com/nurturedandwild

Simon Wooster from Wooster's Bakery www.woostersbakery.co.uk

Andrew Nicolas and Alice Vuap for all the photos taken in Cyprus; we would have loved to be there for those but were not able to due to the Covid-19 pandemic.

Emily Reed www.emilyreedphotography.com for letting us use her photo of Lindsey Kennedy's Dark Chocolate and Orange Cake, Julian Eales www.ealesphotography.co.uk and Dominika Scheibinger www.eightysixstudios.co.uk for use of their images.

Thanks also to Stefan Pantazi, Angie Upshall, Shuk-Yee Lee and George Gorringe for their sterling work.

And last but not least, a big thank you to each and every one of our fantastic customers who have supported us since we started in 2014. Thank you so much for your amazing love and encouragement in person and online over all these years; it's your support that kept us going and we are eternally grateful. You're the best!

CONTENTS

ABOUT THIS BOOK

When we sell our olive oil and halloumi at food festivals, people are always asking us how to cook with them and what to use them for. Customers are really keen to get recipe ideas from us, and we often provide step-by-step instructions while standing at the stall! This book is the perfect solution to those questions, and we're so excited to share some of our favourite Mediterranean recipes for everyday meals, snacks and treats with customers old and new.

We also wanted to create something that would bring together all the people who are involved in OliveOlive, from longstanding fans here in the UK to our friends and family in Cyprus who make the olive oil and halloumi cheese. Putting Pam's family recipes together has been nostalgic, as she remembers her Yiayia Aphrodite and her words of wisdom as she taught Pam how to cook. 'Yiayia' is Greek for grandmother, and yes, Aphrodite was her real name!

Our customers are really interested in the authenticity of our products - the kind of milk used in halloumi, the traditional handmade methods, the annual olive harvest - so we've explained how the halloumi and olive oil go from raw ingredients in Cyprus to being the best part of your dinner. Alongside the recipes, you'll discover the story of OliveOlive and get a real insight into the processes and people that make what we do unique.

Many of the recipes featured in this book come from our own kitchen, but some have been generously shared by friends, family, and a selection of local chefs from some fantastic restaurants who use our products regularly. This is a cookbook for everyone; the recipes are easy to follow, with a few to challenge the more ambitious cooks, and can be whipped up in your home kitchen with minimal equipment. Our food is rustic and full of flavour, with simple steps to delicious dishes.

We hope you enjoy reading and cooking from this book, as well as the most important part: loving our olive oil and halloumi as much as we do!

ABOUT OLIVEOLIVE

We started OliveOlive in 2014 after Rob decided to quit the rat race and fancied trying something completely different. We had no plan whatsoever so we were really stepping into the unknown. Being from Cyprus, Pam had grown up on the family's olive oil. Whenever she gave it to friends they were amazed at how good it tasted compared to the usual supermarket options, so we decided to try selling the family's olive oil to the good people of Cambridgeshire.

For the first few years we were filling empty bottles on the kitchen table and storing hundreds of litres of olive oil in the garden shed, but before long we took a unit near home and the actual filling of the bottles is now done for us in Cyprus.

We were often asked if we could supply halloumi cheese as well, so we started offering authentic, handmade halloumi made by our friends in Cyprus, the Stefani family, who happen to make the best halloumi money can buy. It's the only halloumi Pam's mum buys back in Cyprus, and as Rob says, "you don't argue with your Greek mother-in-law!" This combination of high quality olive oil and traditional halloumi cheese seemed a nice fit, and soon the brand name Cyprus Village was born to reflect our halloumi's authentic heritage.

The business's main source of income usually comes from selling direct to the public at markets and food festivals in Cambridgeshire and all the surrounding counties, and we love nothing more than getting in front of our customers at these events. Many of them have been buying from us for years and often become good friends. When we started, we thought we'd only be doing events for a couple of years, but we're still enjoying getting out there and meeting our fantastic customers.

We now supply a few shops and our online business is growing nicely. We send our products up and down the UK, from Cornwall to the Highlands of Scotland and across the Irish Sea to Northern Ireland. We have also supplied some really good restaurants along the way and continue to do so. These include Maison Bleue in Bury St. Edmunds, The Bedford Lodge Hotel in Newmarket, and Cotto in Cambridge among many others. I always tell our customers they are in Michelin star company when they buy our products!

In 2020, both the olive oil and the halloumi each won two gold stars in the world-renowned Great Taste Awards, which means the judges dubbed it above and beyond delicious. We were delighted to receive the awards and have been busy putting those little black and gold stickers on our products ever since to let the world know.

As for the future, who knows? Given the name OliveOlive, we're often asked if we sell olives and we'd love to one day, if we can find a fantastic supplier of course. And we may well consider other ingredients like dried herbs and honey, if the demand is there. Let us know what you'd like to see in our online shop and we'll see if we can make it happen.

In the meantime, we hope to continue sending our OliveOlive oil and Cyprus Village halloumi to all our wonderful customers for many years to come.

ΕΛΑΙΟΛΑΔΑ
ΕΛΑΙΟΤΡΙΒΕΙΑ ΚΑΡΑΓΙΩΡΓΗΣ ΛΤΔ
ΤΗΛ.: 24432970, ΦΑΞ: 24432655
ΑΛΕΘΡΙΚΟ
UP
UP
Olive Olive
Olive Olive
Olive Olive
© Julian Eales www.ealesphotography.co.uk

OUR OLIVE OIL:
FROM APHRODITE TO BLIGHTY

Before we started OliveOlive, we'd always had the family's olive oil sent over from Cyprus to use at home, so had grown accustomed to the quality. It was only when we gave some to friends who loved it so much that we realised just how hard it is to find good quality olive oil in the UK. In fact, seeing how enthusiastic our friends were about it, we decided to try to make a living out of selling it ourselves.

We visited Pam's family and helped out with the olive harvest to find out what it's all about, and the process is really very simple. The olives are picked by hand, cold-pressed within 24 hours and the resulting extra virgin olive oil is bottled and ready to go. Nothing is added, nothing is taken away: just 100% extra virgin olive oil. We think it's smooth, rich and creamy, without the bitterness you can get in some supermarket versions. We still remember our first olive harvesting experience, and particularly that moment when the pure, fresh extra virgin olive oil pours out of the tap immediately after being pressed. The guys in the mill made toast and when we poured over the oil, it tasted amazing! We often recreate this simple little snack at home: our olive oil on hot toast with a little salt and pepper and a sprinkle of dried herbs, and it's always delicious.

We started selling the olive oil on market stalls and in a few shops, where it proved popular. So much so that after a while we needed more olives! Now the olive oil comes from not only our family's farm in Larnaca, but also from local smallholders and independent olive growers in the region. We're often asked what type of olives are used and the answer we always give is 'the Cyprus olive' which is a little olive indigenous to Cyprus, grown all over the island. Luckily, this variety makes for a deliciously smooth olive oil, without any bitterness, and is high in polyphenols which are really good for you.

We also supply some fantastic restaurants with our olive oil, and in 2020 it won two gold stars in the prestigious Great Taste Awards. One of the judges described the oil as "light on the palate with good grassy notes and a freshness that develops into a pleasing creaminess. Buttery with a hint of pepper at the finish." But our customers don't need awards to know how good it is; just one try is all it takes!

CYPRUS VILLAGE HALLOUMI:
NOT YOUR AVERAGE SQUEAKY CHEESE!

As soon as we told our customers where our olive oil comes from, we got requests to start selling proper Cypriot halloumi cheese. Anybody who'd spent time in Cyprus wasn't satisfied with the usual rubbery synthetic variety in UK supermarkets, so this was a great opportunity to offer them the real deal. Pam asked the family back home who made the best halloumi in Cyprus and that was that; we started a relationship with our original suppliers which continues to this day. Like us, they are a small family business who are passionate about their fantastic halloumi, and absolute sticklers for doing things the traditional way.

Using the OliveOlive brand for the halloumi didn't quite seem to fit, so after some head scratching Pam's daughter Chloe came up with the name Cyprus Village, and it stuck. We also used a picture of Pam's dad's village, Arsos, on the packaging, taken from an old photograph. Arsos is in the Limassol district and just a few miles from Pachna, where our halloumi is made.

As all our customers know, Cyprus Village halloumi is handmade the traditional way with 100% goat's milk, unlike the typical supermarket version which is mass produced with mostly cow's milk. Using cow's milk makes it cheaper but the end result is rubbery, synthetic and bland in flavour...like chewing on a flip flop! We have to pay a little more for ours, but the end result is worth it: deliciously tasty without that plasticky mouthfeel...the best halloumi money can buy.

We're delighted to say that our customers come back to us for this stuff time and time again, and we also supply our halloumi to some fantastic restaurants who pride themselves on buying only the very best ingredients for their customers. In 2020, Cyprus Village halloumi was awarded two gold stars at the world-renowned Great Taste Awards. Our halloumi was described by the panel as "delicious: not rubbery, just soft and creamy. The level of salt is perfect. When grilled, the natural sugar within the milk caramelised to a nutty brown and just added to the overall experience. Delightful." We're so thankful to our wonderful customers too, who've submitted around 400 fantastic reviews so far and are clearly in agreement with the judges!

PROPER
HALLOUMI
CHEESE

Halloumi Cheese

© Julian Eales www.ealesphotography.co.uk

STARTERS, SALADS & SIDES

A TRIO OF HOUMOUS

MAKES 500ML OF EACH | PREPARATION TIME: 10 MINUTES EACH

Homemade houmous is easier than you think, especially if you use tinned chickpeas. You can play about with different flavours like roasted aubergines or beetroot, but here are three classics in our family.

INGREDIENTS

Plain Houmous

400g tinned chickpeas

2 cloves of garlic

1 lemon, juiced

2 heaped tsp tahini

6 tbsp extra virgin olive oil

Lemon and Coriander Houmous

400g tinned chickpeas

2 cloves of garlic

1 lemon, zested and juiced

2 heaped tsp tahini

6 tbsp extra virgin olive oil

60g fresh coriander

Sweet Chilli Houmous

400g tinned chickpeas

1 lemon, juiced

2 heaped tsp tahini

6 tbsp Fused Chilli Oil

2 tbsp sweet chilli sauce

Pinch of chilli flakes (optional, if you like it hot)

METHOD

Drain the chickpeas and throw them into a food processor. Grate or crush in the garlic if using, then add the lemon juice (and zest, for lemon and coriander houmous) and tahini.

Turn on the food processor and drizzle in the olive or chilli oil as everything blends. You may end up using more than 6 tablespoons but who's counting?!

Lastly, add the extras depending on what type of houmous you are making (fresh coriander, sweet chilli sauce and chilli flakes, if using) then taste to check the seasoning.

Chill before serving.

BLACK OLIVE TAPENADE

MAKES 4-5 JARS | PREPARATION TIME: 20 MINUTES

This is our friend Anita's recipe, and it is by far the best tapenade we have ever tasted. She first made it for us many years ago using our family's olive oil and we have loved it ever since. This is the perfect gift to make for friends.

INGREDIENTS

450g pitted black olives

100g fresh basil with stalks, washed

80g sun-dried tomatoes

45g capers

8 anchovies

6 cloves of garlic, peeled

2-3 tbsp oil from sun-dried tomatoes

½ tsp chilli flakes

½ tsp caster sugar

Sea salt and black pepper

50ml extra virgin olive oil

METHOD

Place all the ingredients into a food processor and blitz until you reach your preferred consistency. Adjust the seasoning to taste and mix well.

Spoon the tapenade into sterilised jars, leaving some space at the top for an extra drizzle of olive oil before sealing with a lid.

Best stored in a refrigerator, this keeps for up to 2 weeks when sealed.

ANITA KEARNS

BUTTER BEAN DIP

MAKES 500ML | PREPARATION TIME: 10 MINUTES

This is another recipe from our friend Anita. It came about when she wanted to make houmous but had no chickpeas in her larder! So, having a few tins of butter beans instead, she decided to use them and realised that the humble butter bean makes a delicious creamy dip.

INGREDIENTS

400g tinned butter beans

3 cloves of garlic

2 tbsp tahini

½ a lemon, juiced

Sea salt and black pepper

80ml extra virgin olive oil

60ml warm water

Sprinkle of sumac

METHOD

Drain the tinned beans and peel the cloves of garlic, then place all the ingredients except the sumac in a food processor and blitz until smooth.

Add a little more oil if needed to get the right consistency for your dip. Pour into a container such as a Mason jar, sprinkle with sumac and drizzle with more olive oil.

Cover the container with a lid and keep the dip refrigerated. It keeps well for up to 5 days.

PATATOSALATA ME AVYA
(CYPRIOT POTATO SALAD WITH EGGS)

SERVES 4 | PREPARATION TIME: 15 MINUTES | COOKING TIME: 15 MINUTES

My mum made this after our Easter egg-cracking competition, called tsougrisma. Traditionally, hard-boiled dyed eggs were used for the game. My brother once used our mum's red nail varnish to make his egg stronger! You can eat this salad warm or cold, even the next day if refrigerated overnight.

INGREDIENTS

1kg baby new potatoes

5 eggs

Splash of vinegar

1 lemon, juiced

10g chives, or 5 spring onions

Handful of fresh coriander, finely chopped

4 tbsp extra virgin olive oil

Sea salt and black pepper

METHOD

Cut the potatoes into halves or quarters so they are all roughly the same size. Place in a pan and cover with cold water. Bring to the boil then simmer for 10 to 15 minutes. The potatoes are ready when they feel soft if poked with a sharp knife.

Meanwhile, put the eggs into another saucepan. Cover them with cold water and add a splash of vinegar; this stops them from cracking while cooking. Gently bring to the boil then simmer for 7 minutes. Transfer them into a bowl and place straight under a cold running tap. Leave the eggs to cool slightly before peeling.

Drain the potatoes, add to a bowl, and squeeze over the lemon juice to stop them from discolouring. Peel the eggs, chop them roughly and add to the potatoes. Use scissors to cut the chives into the bowl. If you are using spring onions, discard most of the green part and finely chop the rest. My mum used spring onions, but I prefer the subtle flavour of the chives.

Add the chopped coriander and drizzle over the olive oil. Season to taste and stir well so that the egg and olive oil mix together, creating a creamy texture.

CYPRUS CHIPS

SERVES 4 | PREPARATION TIME: 10 MINUTES | COOKING TIME: 45 MINUTES

The best chips are made with Cyprus potatoes, of course! We've tried other varieties, and while they are nice, we prefer these. My Yiayia (grandmother) always fried them in olive oil and believe me, they taste amazing. My own tip is parboiling them; it's definitely worth the extra washing up!

INGREDIENTS

5 large Cyprus potatoes, peeled

Sea salt and black pepper

350ml extra virgin olive oil

METHOD

Peel and cut the potatoes into similar sized chip shapes. Place them in a large saucepan, add enough cold water to cover the potatoes and bring to the boil.

Simmer for 10 minutes, then drain the potatoes and season well with salt and pepper. Pour the oil into a deep pan on a high heat. You'll need to work out how long it takes for the oil to get to the right temperature depending on your hob. Test this by putting one chip in the pan; if it sizzles and rises, carefully add the remaining chips, making sure they are all immersed in the oil.

Slightly reduce the heat and avoid the temptation to turn the chips for 10 minutes, as turning too soon will break them. After 10 minutes, use a spoon to gently release the chips from the bottom and sides of the pan. If they do not come away easily, leave for a few more minutes.

The chips should be ready after about 30 minutes in total, and will need turning occasionally to make sure they cook evenly. When they are golden in colour, use a slotted spoon to transfer them to a plate lined with kitchen roll to absorb the excess oil before serving.

EASY PESTO DRESSING

We like pesto as a dressing on salads as well as with pasta. You can whizz this up in minutes. We make ours dairy-free, but you could add some grated parmesan or pecorino to the ingredients before you blend everything together.

INGREDIENTS

100ml extra virgin olive oil

Small bunch of basil leaves (about 30g)

15g pine nuts

2 cloves of garlic

1 lemon or lime, juiced

Sea salt and black pepper

METHOD

Put all the ingredients into a large jug or cup and use a handheld blender to whizz everything together. Season to taste.

MARTA WIERZBICKA

GRILLED HALLOUMI SALAD

SERVES 4-6 | PREPARATION TIME: 15 MINUTES | COOKING TIME: 40 MINUTES

Marta is a good friend and a big fan of all things OliveOlive. She is a keen and excellent cook. This recipe is simple but delicious and perfect for outdoor dining. Marta likes to cook all the vegetables with the halloumi on the barbecue, if the weather allows!

INGREDIENTS

1 large or 2 small aubergines

1 large or 2 small courgettes

Red, yellow, and orange peppers

6-8 open cup mushrooms

250g halloumi

Generous drizzle of olive oil

Sea salt and black pepper

Chilli flakes, garlic powder, dried basil, dried oregano (optional)

Sprig of fresh rosemary (optional)

Fresh parsley, to garnish

METHOD

First, prepare the vegetables. Slice the aubergine and courgette into rounds about 1cm thick. Halve the peppers and remove their cores, seeds and white membranes. If liked, peel the skin off the mushrooms. Lastly, cut the halloumi into slices about 0.5cm thick.

Lay all the prepared vegetables and halloumi on a baking tray and drizzle with the olive oil, then season with salt and pepper. Sprinkle over some dried herbs or other flavourings of your choice.

Place the tray under a hot grill to cook until everything is golden brown on both sides. You could also do this on a barbecue. If you like, add the fresh rosemary to the tray while cooking.

When the vegetables are ready, let everything cool down a little. Peel the skin off the peppers, then slice them into bite-size chunks.

Chop the rest of the veggies into bite-size chunks if needed and arrange them on a platter. Place the halloumi on the top and garnish the salad with a little fresh parsley.

HALLOUMI AND WATERMELON APPETISERS

MAKES 24 APPETISERS | PREPARATION TIME: 15 MINUTES

This is more a tip than a recipe, but for as long as I can remember my favourite summer breakfast and snack has been watermelon and halloumi. You can use this same combination to make some lovely, posh-looking appetisers on cocktail sticks with the addition of fresh mint.

INGREDIENTS

1 watermelon

250g halloumi

24 mint leaves

24 cocktail sticks

METHOD

You won't need the whole watermelon, so cut off a piece and dice the flesh into 24 similar sized cubes. Cut the halloumi into 24 similar sized cubes and have the mint leaves handy.

To assemble the appetisers, stack up a cube of halloumi, a mint leaf in the middle and a watermelon cube on the top. Pierce this trio with a cocktail stick and repeat 23 more times!

This also works well with halved cherry or baby plum tomatoes and basil leaves.

Alternatively, simply put some watermelon chunks with a few slices or cubes of halloumi straight from the pack into a bowl for the easiest summer lunch or snack. Then you can mop up the sweet and salty juice with some bread or, like the five-year-old me, just drink it from the bowl!

HALLOUMI FRIES WITH POMEGRANATE, SPRING ONION AND CORIANDER

SERVES 3-4 | PREPARATION TIME: 10 MINUTES | COOKING TIME: 10 MINUTES

If you've ever had the famous halloumi fries at The Crown Inn, Broughton, you'll know exactly how delicious they are, and here's the recipe straight from the head chef himself, Mark Frith. Remember to use only the best Cyprus Village halloumi cheese for full flavour!

INGREDIENTS

250g halloumi

Gram (chickpea) flour or cornflour

1 pomegranate

A few spring onions

Fresh coriander

1 lemon, juiced

100ml mayonnaise

Pomegranate molasses

METHOD

Cut the block of halloumi into chip-sized fingers, then shake enough flour to dust all the halloumi into a tray. Roll the fingers in the flour until thoroughly coated.

To prepare the garnish, deseed the pomegranate by halving it, holding one half cut side down in your hand with your fingers slightly spread, then firmly tapping the fruit over a bowl until all the seeds have fallen out. Wash the spring onions, then slice on the diagonal. Roughly chop the fresh coriander. Stir some of the lemon juice into the mayonnaise and taste to see whether you are happy with the flavour. Add more lemon juice or a little water until the mixture is a salad dressing consistency.

Once everything is ready, heat a deep fat fryer to 180°c. Alternatively, use a large saucepan half filled with oil, but please only do this if you have a thermometer.

Shake the excess flour off the halloumi fingers, then carefully place them into the hot oil. Move them around gently until golden brown, and don't take your eyes off them as they can darken fast. When the fries are ready, transfer them onto a tray lined with kitchen paper to drain off the oil and help them stay crisp.

To plate the halloumi fries, arrange them mostly in one layer so everything gets an even helping of toppings. Drizzle over some pomegranate molasses (if you don't have any or prefer not to use it, balsamic vinegar can be used here instead) then sprinkle the halloumi fries with the pomegranate seeds and spring onion. Finish with the lemon mayonnaise and a scattering of fresh coriander.

HALLOUMI WITH CAPONATA AND PESTO

SERVES 2 | PREPARATION TIME: 15 MINUTES | COOKING TIME: 1 HOUR 30 MINUTES

Maria says: "This dish was based on a delicious burrata I had at the top of a Swiss mountain. With halloumi, the combination of salty, sweet, slightly sharp and creamy flavours is extremely satisfying. The Cyprus Village halloumi from OliveOlive has a superior taste and texture to any other halloumi I've tasted."

INGREDIENTS

1 block of Cyprus Village halloumi

For the caponata

Extra virgin olive oil (from OliveOlive of course!)

3 medium aubergines, cut into 1.5cm dice

2 red onions or 4 large shallots, peeled and diced

30g caster sugar

6 stalks of celery, cut into 0.5cm dice

Generous handful of capers

3 cloves of garlic, finely chopped

1.5kg cherry tomatoes

100ml red wine vinegar

Sea salt and black pepper

Handful of basil leaves

For the pesto

50g pine nuts, plus extra for garnish

50g parmesan or vegetarian alternative, diced

80g basil (reserve tips for garnish)

150ml extra virgin olive oil

2 cloves of garlic

METHOD

For the caponata

Preheat the oven to 160°c/140°c fan/Gas Mark 3. Heat the oil in a heavy-based, preferably non-stick pan and fry the diced aubergine in batches. This way you don't lose the heat and they will brown nicely. Drain the fried aubergine on kitchen paper to absorb the excess oil, as aubergines can soak up quite a bit.

Add the onions to the pan with a little more oil if needed. Fry gently until softened, then add the caster sugar and allow the onions to caramelise. Add the diced celery and capers, cook until soft and glossy, then transfer the mixture to a roasting tray.

Stir in the cooked aubergine, scatter over the garlic and cherry tomatoes, then pour the red wine vinegar over the mixture. Season with salt and pepper then place the tray in the preheated oven. Cook for around 1 hour, until the mixture stops looking watery but the tomatoes still have some shape. Give everything a good stir then tear over the basil leaves and fold them in. This makes quite a generous portion, but it freezes beautifully and is also delicious with lamb.

For the pesto

Toast all the pine nuts in a dry pan over a medium heat, or on a tray in the oven. Put 50g into a blender, liquidiser or small food processor. Blitz until quite smooth but with colour and texture. Add the cheese, basil, olive oil and garlic then blitz again to your preferred consistency.

To cook the halloumi, either heat a griddle pan without oil, or heat a little oil in a non-stick frying pan. Slice or cube the halloumi, then place it into the pan to griddle or fry over a medium heat. It should soften and brown but not spread.

Place the caponata on the plates, layer on the halloumi, then spoon over the pesto. It is very pungent so don't go mad! Garnish with the basil tips and a scattering of pine nuts that give a fabulous crunch. The remaining pesto is great with pasta!

PASCAL CANEVET (MAISON BLEUE, BURY ST. EDMUNDS)
WWW.MAISONBLEUE.CO.UK

HEIRLOOM TOMATO CARPACCIO WITH OLIVE OIL ICE CREAM

SERVES 4 | PREPARATION TIME: 20-30 MINUTES, PLUS OVERNIGHT | COOKING TIME: 5-10 MINUTES

Pascal says: "Tomatoes are relatively easy to grow and the rewards are delicious. This easy recipe makes a pretty summer dish for you to enjoy and share with friends. The olive ice cream has a creamy, silky texture with a saltiness that enhances every delicious mouthful."

INGREDIENTS

For the olive oil ice cream

250ml hot milk

100ml olive oil

4 eggs yolks

150g caster sugar

75g black olive purée

For the carpaccio

1 pineapple tomato (a yellow and red beefsteak tomato)

4 large heirloom Noir de Crimée tomatoes

2 plum tomatoes

3 tbsp extra virgin olive oil

Sea salt and black pepper

Pinch of madras curry powder

METHOD

For the olive oil ice cream

Bring the milk and the olive oil to the boil in a saucepan, stir and remove from the heat. Whisk the egg yolks and sugar together until pale and smooth. Gradually add this mixture to the pan of milk and oil in a steady stream, whisking continuously. Cook on a gentle medium heat until the mixture has thickened enough to coat the back of a wooden spoon, about 2 to 3 minutes. Strain the custard through a sieve into a clean bowl set inside a bowl of cold iced water then whisk in the black olive purée. Let it cool, season to taste, then churn and chill the mixture in an ice cream machine. Transfer the ice cream into an airtight container, cover and freeze until firm.

For the carpaccio

Carefully core the tomatoes from the top, keeping them whole, and bring a pan of water to the boil. Plunge the tomatoes into the boiling water and leave for 15 to 20 seconds, then transfer them into ice cold water. Gently peel off the skins when cool and leave to drain. Quarter the peeled tomatoes and remove the seeded parts, keeping them for later. Arrange the pieces on a baking tray lined with greaseproof paper. Drizzle with olive oil, season with salt and pepper, then sandwich the tomatoes with another layer of greaseproof paper and another tray. Place some kitchen weights on top and refrigerate overnight to gently squeeze the juices out. Meanwhile, combine the seeded tomato insides, a tablespoon of olive oil and the curry powder. Season to taste then chill.

To serve

Use a large ring to plate the tomatoes, arranging them and mixing the vibrant colours. Remove the ring and carefully add a quenelle of the black olive ice cream, then finish with the curry dressing. Voilà.

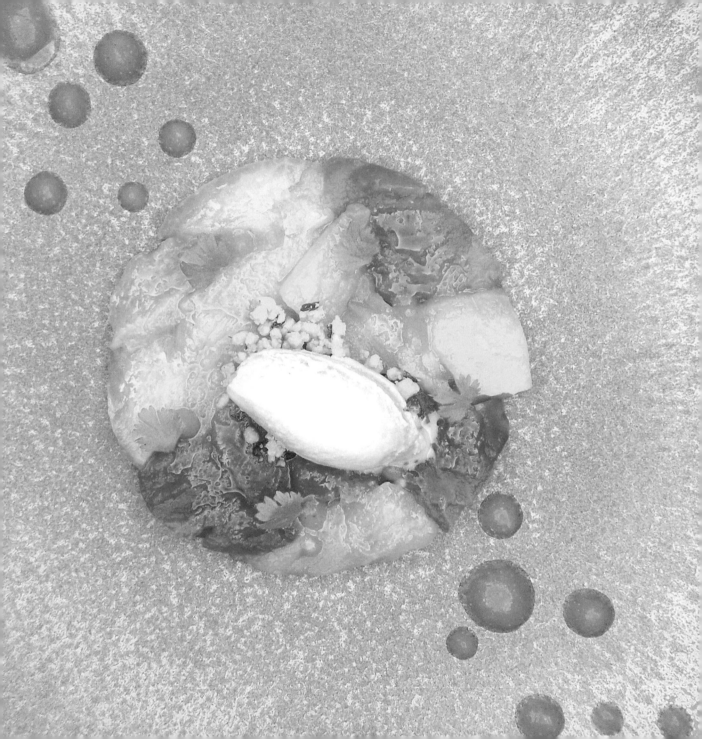

LENTIL TABBOULEH WITH SEARED HALLOUMI, CANDIED WALNUTS & POMEGRANATE DRESSING

SERVES 4 | PREPARATION TIME: 15 MINUTES | COOKING TIME: 15 MINUTES, PLUS 20 MINUTES IF USING DRIED LENTILS

Scott says: "The Stove in Bourn, Cambridgeshire is an independently run coffee shop and café in the countryside. We pride ourselves on using local producers and suppliers. All our produce is homemade. The recipe below is a very popular dish on our menu and we hope you enjoy it."

INGREDIENTS

200g dried or 400g tinned Puy lentils

Bunch of fresh mint, roughly chopped

Bunch of fresh flat parsley, roughly chopped

Bunch of spring onions, finely chopped

8-10 cherry tomatoes, halved

50g walnuts

1 tbsp honey

1 block of halloumi, sliced

1 lemon

Generous drizzle of extra virgin olive oil

Drizzle of pomegranate molasses

Lettuce leaves

METHOD

If you're using dried lentils, rinse them in cold water and then cook in a pan of simmering water until tender. Drain and set to one side.

Put the herbs, spring onions and cherry tomatoes into a large mixing bowl. Drizzle the walnuts with the honey and gently caramelise in the oven or in a frying pan. Allow to cool.

Heat a small amount of olive oil in another pan and cook the halloumi on each side for 2 to 3 minutes. Allow the halloumi to drain while keeping it warm.

Add the cooked or tinned lentils to the bowl of herbs, spring onions and cherry tomatoes. Dress the mixture with freshly squeezed lemon juice and a drizzle of extra virgin olive oil. Gently stir everything together and season to taste.

Serve the salad in a large bowl with a few lettuce leaves. Sprinkle with the caramelised walnuts, add the warm halloumi and drizzle some pomegranate molasses over the top before serving.

Chef's Tip: If you can't get pomegranate molasses, you can reduce pomegranate juice over a medium heat until the liquid is a third of its original volume and has a syrupy consistency.

GEORGIA SOLOMONIDES

MELITZANOSALATA (AUBERGINE DIP)

MAKES 500ML | PREPARATION TIME: 15 MINUTES | COOKING TIME: 25 MINUTES

This is my Theia (aunt) Georgia's recipe for melitzanosalata, which in my opinion is the best version I have ever had. It's a delicious snack served with warmed pitta bread and vegetable sticks.

INGREDIENTS

2 aubergines (approximately 500g)

50ml extra virgin olive oil

1 lemon, juiced

1 tsp sea salt

2 heaped tsp wholegrain mustard

1 heaped tbsp mayonnaise

2 cloves of garlic, grated or crushed

METHOD

Preheat the oven to 220°c/200°c fan/Gas Mark 7.

Cut the stalks off the aubergines, prick them on all sides with a sharp knife and place on a baking tray. Roast the aubergines in the preheated oven for 25 minutes, or until they shrink and go soft. Remove from the oven and leave to cool.

When the aubergines are cool enough to touch, peel them and slice them lengthways into quarters. Place the quarters into a food processor and blitz until smooth. With the food processor running, add the olive oil, lemon juice, salt, mustard, mayonnaise, and garlic.

Pour the dip into a jar and chill in the fridge. This should keep for about a week in the fridge and in an airtight jar.

ROSEMARY AND SEA SALT FOCACCIA

MAKES 1 X 20 BY 25CM LOAF | PREPARATION TIME: 1 HOUR 30 MINUTES | COOKING TIME: 25 MINUTES

Simon Wooster says: "Focaccia comes in many variations and styles, but cold-pressed olive oil is the key ingredient in these classic Italian bakes. This recipe makes a light, bubbly and open-textured bread thanks to the high water content, so a food mixer with a dough hook is handy if you have one."

INGREDIENTS

300g strong bread flour

½ a sachet of dried instant yeast

5g fine salt

230g tepid water

Olive oil

Sea salt flakes

Small bunch of fresh rosemary, leaves picked

METHOD

Mix the flour, yeast and salt together, then add about 200g of the water. Knead into a dough then gradually add the remaining water. It will seem impossibly wet, but persevere until the very soft dough is smooth and shiny.

If you are kneading by hand, it pays to knead for 5 minutes and then let it rest for 10 minutes, repeating until the dough has developed. If you're using a food mixer, gradually add the water on medium speed and then mix fast for a few minutes. When you hear the dough slapping against the mixing bowl, it's ready. Using the dough function on a breadmaker will also work, providing you still add the water gradually: start with 200g and add the remaining 30g half way through the kneading cycle.

Oil a non-stick baking tray; one at least 3cm deep and roughly 20 by 25cm will suit this recipe. Tip your dough into it, pushing into the corners until it's a roughly even depth all over.

Leave it to rise for 1 hour, then preheat the oven to about 215°c/195°c fan/Gas Mark 7 to 8. Drizzle the surface of the dough with olive oil. Push your fingertips firmly into the dough to create dimples – these will fill up with the oil – and then sprinkle the focaccia with the sea salt flakes and rosemary leaves according to taste.

Bake the focaccia in the preheated oven for about 25 minutes. Once done, lightly drizzle your focaccia with more olive oil, then cut into squares and serve.

TRADITIONAL CYPRIOT SALAD WITH RED WINE VINEGAR DRESSING

SERVES 4 | PREPARATION TIME: 10-15 MINUTES

Depending on personal preference, Cypriot salads are dressed with a vinegar- or lemon-based dressing. My dad makes his own red wine vinegar, so we always use that. This is the basic recipe, but you can add halloumi, olives, feta, capers, rocket, radish... anything you like!

INGREDIENTS

6 lettuce leaves (romaine or cos lettuce works best)

2 medium tomatoes

½ a cucumber

For the red wine vinegar dressing

3 tbsp extra virgin olive oil

1 tbsp red wine vinegar

Sea salt and black pepper

METHOD

Arrange the lettuce, tomatoes and cucumber, chopped how you like them, on a plate.

For the red wine vinegar dressing

Put all ingredients into a jar, place the lid on and shake. Taste and season to your liking. The measures here are approximate; we usually just pour and taste as we go along!

Drizzle the dressing over the salad and serve.

MAIN MEALS

AUTUMNAL RISOTTO WITH HALLOUMI

SERVES 6 | PREPARATION TIME: 15 MINUTES | COOKING TIME: 1 HOUR

This is a family favourite and an easy one pan meal that looks quite impressive if you are entertaining. We named it autumnal risotto because of the colours, but you can of course make it any time of the year!

INGREDIENTS

2 medium sweet potatoes

2 medium courgettes

2 yellow peppers

1 leek

2 tbsp extra virgin olive oil

Freshly ground mixed peppercorns

350g long grain rice

800g tinned lentils

800ml vegetable stock

120ml white wine

250g halloumi, cubed

Chopped fresh parsley, to garnish

METHOD

Preheat the oven to 200°c/180°c fan/Gas Mark 6. Prepare all the vegetables by cutting them into similar sized cubes. Cut the leek lengthways into quarters and then slice.

Place the vegetables into a deep roasting tray and drizzle over the olive oil. Add a generous amount of pepper (but no salt, as you may find it salty enough once you have added the halloumi and stock).

Place the roasting tin, uncovered, on the middle shelf of the oven for 25 minutes. Remove it from the oven, drain off any liquid, then add the rice, lentils, stock, wine and halloumi to the roasted vegetables.

Stir everything well, cover the tin with foil and then put it back in the oven for 35 minutes or until the rice is cooked. Check and stir halfway through the cooking time.

Garnish the risotto with fresh parsley and serve.

GEORGE UPSHALL
@NURTUREDANDWILD

BUTTER ROASTED MONKFISH WITH CLAMS AND COURGETTE

SERVES 4 | PREPARATION TIME: 30 MINUTES | COOKING TIME: 15 MINUTES

George says: "Monkfish is best treated like a piece of meat when it comes to cooking, roasted on the bone then rested well. Choose small firm courgettes for a salad which stands up well to the richness of the almonds and the sweet, salty clams. Best enjoyed in the late summer months."

INGREDIENTS

4 small monkfish tails around 400g each, or a 1.5kg fillet

400g live clams, washed

50g unsalted butter

For the almond pesto

100g smoked almonds

1 clove of garlic

1 sprig of thyme

60ml olive oil

For the almond sauce

100g smoked almonds

1 tbsp olive oil

200ml almond milk or whole cow's milk

For the courgette salad

4 small courgettes

Sea salt

½ a lemon

1 sprig of lemon verbena

METHOD

For the almond pesto

Lightly toast the smoked almonds in a dry pan for a few minutes. Cool then roughly chop the almonds and finely chop the garlic and thyme. Combine them with the oil, then add salt to taste.

For the almond sauce

Blend the ingredients together, then leave to infuse for 10 minutes. Wrap the mixture in a piece of muslin cloth and squeeze over a bowl, extracting as much liquid as possible. The almonds left in the cloth can be added to the pesto.

For the courgette salad

Finely slice the courgettes then season with a little salt, a good squeeze of lemon juice and some finely chopped lemon verbena.

To cook the fish, heat the butter in a nonstick frying pan until it begins to foam, season the monkfish with salt and carefully place in the pan. Baste the fish in the butter as it cooks. Once you have a nice colour on one side, flip the fish over and reduce the heat a little. Continue to baste in the butter, which should now be a nut brown colour. The fish is done when a skewer inserted close to the bone at the thickest part comes out with very little resistance. Remove the fish from the pan and leave to rest. Put the same pan back on a high heat, then add the clams and cover with a lid. Cook for 3 to 4 minutes, shaking the pan occasionally until the clams pop open. Remove the clams with a slotted spoon, then reduce the juices by half, turn off the heat and pour in your almond sauce.

To serve

Arrange the courgette salad on your plates, carve the rested monkfish (if using one piece) and place a portion on each. Surround with the clams and finish the dish with a spoonful of pesto and almond sauce.

COUSIN COSTAS' KLEFTIKO
(SLOW COOKED LEG OF LAMB)

SERVES 4-6 | PREPARATION TIME: 10 MINUTES | COOKING TIME: 2 HOURS 30 MINUTES

Kleftiko means 'stolen'. It originated in Greece from the 14th century, when mountain guerillas would steal a lamb or goat and cook it in underground pits to avoid detection from smoke or the smell of the cooking. This is my cousin Costas' recipe which he has kindly let me share.

INGREDIENTS

1 leg of lamb

1 onion, peeled and sliced into rings

2 tbsp extra virgin olive oil

3 cloves of garlic, crushed

4 bay leaves

1 tbsp dried oregano

1 tbsp dried thyme

1 tsp ground cinnamon

300ml water

Sea salt and black pepper

METHOD

Preheat the oven to 160°c/140°c fan/Gas Mark 3. Put all the ingredients into a large, deep roasting tray.

Cover the tray with foil and slow roast in the preheated oven for 2 hours 30 minutes. The meat should separate easily from the bone and melt in your mouth.

Serve the kleftiko with a nice big dollop of Greek yoghurt and a Cypriot salad on the side. You can also add potatoes to the recipe; peel a couple, slice them into discs then add them to the roasting tray with everything else. They absorb all the flavours from the lamb and taste delicious.

FAKES
(CYPRIOT STYLE LENTILS)

SERVES 4 | PREPARATION TIME: 10 MINUTES | COOKING TIME: 45 MINUTES

Most Cypriots will know this traditional dish as faggi. This recipe uses dried lentils, but you can use tinned ones as a cheat; just remember to add the water when you add the rice. This dish goes well with grilled meat, fish, or a salad of tomatoes, onions, and cucumber.

INGREDIENTS

265g green or brown lentils

150g basmati rice

850ml cold water

½ a lemon, juiced

1 tsp vegetable stock powder

150ml extra virgin olive oil

2 onions, thinly sliced

Sea salt and black pepper

Handful of Kalamata olives (optional)

METHOD

First, rinse the lentils and rice separately in a sieve under cold running water. Place the washed lentils in a deep pan then add the water, lemon juice and stock powder (this prevents the lentils from turning black and flavours them nicely). Place over a medium heat, bring to the boil and simmer until lentils soften. This should take about 20 minutes but cooking times can vary and the lentils should be just al dente.

In another saucepan, heat the olive oil and gently fry one of the sliced onions with a pinch of salt until pale and soft. Remove from the heat and set aside.

Add the washed rice to the softened lentils and cook for a minute over a low heat. Add the sautéed onion then simmer until the rice is cooked and the excess water has evaporated. You may need to add a little water if the rice or lentils need longer to cook.

Season the rice and lentil mixture to taste, then remove the pan from the heat, add a drizzle of olive oil and cover.

Fry the remaining sliced onion in a drizzle of olive oil for 5 minutes on a medium heat, then add the olives and fry for a further 5 to 10 minutes until the onions are crispy.

Place the fakes in a serving dish and garnish with the crispy onions and olives.

FASOLAKIA YIAHNI

(FINE GREEN BEANS IN TOMATO SAUCE, WITH CHICKEN AND POTATOES)

SERVES 4 | PREPARATION TIME: 10 MINUTES | COOKING TIME: 1 HOUR 15 MINUTES

Anything 'yiahni', meaning with a tomato sauce, goes well with potatoes. This recipe uses large potatoes, peeled and cut into small pieces, but you can use baby new potatoes with the skin on.

INGREDIENTS

8 skinless and boneless chicken thighs, sliced into strips

Generous drizzle of extra virgin olive oil

2 white onions, finely chopped

2-3 cloves of garlic, grated

1 cinnamon stick

1 bay leaf

4-5 carrots, thickly sliced

500g potatoes, peeled and cubed

1 tbsp tomato purée

1 tbsp red wine vinegar

600g fresh or frozen green beans (if fresh, trim the ends)

400g passata

600ml chicken or vegetable stock

Sea salt and black pepper

METHOD

Place a large saucepan over a medium heat, then seal the chicken strips in a generous drizzle of olive oil. Transfer the chicken to a plate and set aside.

Using the same pan, gently sauté the chopped onions and garlic. Add the cinnamon stick, bay leaf and a pinch of salt, then add the carrots and potatoes. Cook for 5 minutes.

Stir in the tomato purée and red wine vinegar, cook for a further 2 to 3 minutes, then stir in the green beans, coating them in the sauce. Add the passata and stir thoroughly before adding the stock.

Put the chicken strips back in the pan, stir well, cover with a lid and simmer for about 1 hour. Stir occasionally and when the sauce has thickened, the potatoes are cooked through and the beans are soft, season the mixture with sea salt and black pepper to taste.

This recipe can also be made with lamb or pork, or without meat altogether. If you are not using meat, you will only need to simmer the mixture for up to 40 minutes after adding the stock.

FASOLES YIAHNI
(BEANS IN TOMATO SAUCE)

SERVES 2 | PREPARATION TIME: 10 MINUTES | COOKING TIME: 1 HOUR

I may get told off (by my mum) for this cheat recipe using tinned beans instead of dried, but those with busy lives will appreciate that! If you do use dried beans, you need to soak them overnight, then cook them in fresh water until they are al dente.

INGREDIENTS

1 onion, finely chopped

2 tbsp olive oil

3 carrots

3 large stalks of celery, finely chopped

15g parsley, finely chopped

Sea salt and black pepper

400g tinned chopped tomatoes

2 tsp sugar

500ml vegetable stock

4 medium potatoes, peeled and cut into cubes

400g tinned white kidney beans (also known as cannellini beans)

METHOD

Fry the onion in the olive oil until soft and glossy. Cut the carrots lengthways into quarters then slice and add to the pan. Stir in the chopped celery and parsley then season with sea salt and black pepper. Stir well and cook for a few minutes.

Add the tinned tomatoes and sugar, stir well to coat all the vegetables, then add the stock. Stir in the cubed potato and drain the beans then add them to the pan. Stir so that everything is covered with the sauce.

Simmer the mixture with the lid on but not sealed shut (leaving a slight gap so steam can escape) for about 1 hour, stirring occasionally, then serve.

GREEK STYLE ROAST FISH

SERVES 4 | PREPARATION TIME: 15 MINUTES | COOKING TIME: 50 MINUTES

Sean says: "This is simple, tasty and full of sunshine. It's all about the ingredients, which should be fresh and full of flavour, to make a great family meal. If you prefer, any skinless white fish can be used instead of haddock."

INGREDIENTS

5 small potatoes (about 400g), scrubbed and cut into wedges

1 onion, halved and sliced

2 cloves of garlic, roughly chopped

½ tbsp chopped fresh oregano or ½ tsp dried oregano

3 tbsp olive oil

Sea salt and black pepper

1 lemon, cut into wedges

2 large tomatoes, cut into wedges (or 16 cherry tomatoes)

4 fresh skinless haddock or other white fish fillets (about 400g)

Small handful of fresh parsley, roughly chopped

METHOD

Preheat the oven to 200°c/180°c fan/Gas Mark 6. Tip the potatoes, onion, garlic, oregano and olive oil into a roasting tin, season with salt and pepper, then mix together with your hands to coat the vegetables in the oil.

Place them in the preheated oven to roast for 15 minutes, then turn everything over and bake for 15 more minutes.

After the first 30 minutes, add the lemon and tomato wedges to the tin, and roast for another 10 minutes.

Lastly, place the fish fillets on top of the vegetables and cook for 10 more minutes. Serve with the fresh parsley scattered over everything.

HALLOUMI BURGERS

MAKES 12 | PREPARATION TIME: 15 MINUTES | COOKING TIME: 20-25 MINUTES (OVEN BAKED) OR 10 MINUTES (FRIED)

This was an experiment that paid off. I use a basic keftedes recipe, but instead of making balls, I flatten them into burger shapes. These can be cooked in the oven or fried; they do taste best when fried, but oven baked is almost as good, healthier, and less messy.

INGREDIENTS

250g halloumi, grated

1 medium potato, peeled and grated

1 egg

15g fresh parsley, finely chopped

Black pepper

Handful of dried mint

1 slice of bread

METHOD

Put the grated halloumi and potato into a bowl. Add the egg, parsley and pepper then rub the mint between the palms of your hands to crush it into the bowl. Add the bread; I always blitz it into breadcrumbs in the food processor because I use homemade bread, which is harder, but if you're using shop-bought sliced bread, you can just throw it in.

If you are baking the burgers, preheat the oven to 220°c/200°c fan/Gas Mark 8. Now use your hands to mix and squidge everything together. You should be able to form a ball that stays together. If it's too wet, add a little more bread; if it's too dry, add a little olive oil. Make up the burgers using your hands, rolling into a ball first then flattening into a burger shape.

Place the burgers on a baking tray lined with greaseproof paper. When the oven is hot, bake the burgers for about 20 to 25 minutes, turning them over halfway through the cooking time.

If you are deep frying them, it will take about 10 minutes. I use olive oil (of course) and turn them occasionally. They will be crispy on the outside but soft in the middle.

Serve either in a bun or a warmed pitta, with a salad garnish. You could also serve them with chips and a salad; there are lots of options for these delicious burgers!

HALLOUMI ORZOTTO

SERVES 4 | PREPARATION TIME: 10 MINUTES | COOKING TIME: 30 MINUTES (INCLUDING RESTING TIME)

Orzo (kritharaki in Greek) was my children's favourite meal. When they were little, they liked it made simply with tomato sauce and with grated halloumi as a garnish, but this is my favourite grown-up version.

INGREDIENTS

3 tbsp extra virgin olive oil

1 red onion, finely chopped

2 cloves of garlic, crushed

1 large leek, cut into rounds

1 large courgette, cut into small pieces

1 red pepper, cut into chunks

10 cherry tomatoes, halved

250g halloumi, diced

4 tbsp tomato passata

Big pinch of dried oregano

350g orzo (kritharaki)

Splash of white wine

800ml vegetable stock

Black pepper

Baby spinach leaves

METHOD

Heat the oil in a big pan, then add the onion and garlic to cook gently until the onions have softened. Add the vegetables and cook until they have softened.

Throw in the halloumi, passata and oregano then stir well so that all the vegetables are coated. Add the orzo and stir well. Pour in the wine and stock, then season with some black pepper.

Bring to the boil, then cook on a low heat. Stir regularly to stop the orzo from sticking to the bottom of the pan. If this happens, take the pan off the heat for a moment and stir quickly; the orzo should come away from the bottom of the pan.

After 20 minutes, check that the orzo is cooked to your liking, turn off the heat when it's ready and fold in the spinach. Leave the orzotto to rest before serving, allowing the spinach to wilt and the flavours to come together.

Serve with grated halloumi.

OLA MASKIEWICZ

HALLOUMI, BACON AND BROCCOLI TART

SERVES 6-8 | PREPARATION TIME: 1 HOUR | COOKING TIME: 1 HOUR 10 MINUTES

Ola is passionate about cooking. She loves experimenting with flavours and always makes amazing food.
She loves making tarts so it was only right that this recipe should be included here!
You can follow Ola on Facebook and Instagram @OlaBakesCakes.

INGREDIENTS

For the pastry

200g plain flour

1 tsp icing sugar

½ tsp fine salt

100g unsalted butter, cut into 1cm cubes and chilled

1 egg, beaten

For the filling

4 rashers of bacon

125g halloumi, thinly sliced

10 broccoli florets

2 radishes, thinly sliced

1 small courgette, thinly sliced

10 cherry tomatoes, halved

4 eggs

3 tbsp milk

Sea salt and black pepper

Dried mixed herbs (we used dill and thyme)

Sprinkle of dried garlic

METHOD

For the pastry

Sift the flour into a large bowl with the icing sugar and salt. Add the cold butter and rub the ingredients together with your fingers to make a soft breadcrumb-like texture. Add the egg and stir it in, bringing the mixture together to form a firm dough. Add a tiny splash of cold water if required. Gently press the pastry into a smooth ball, then refrigerate for 30 minutes.

Roll out the chilled pastry on a lightly floured surface and use it to line a well-buttered 22cm flan dish. Don't cut the overhanging edges off yet, and place the tart base back in the fridge for 20 minutes. Meanwhile, preheat the oven to 180°c/160°c fan/Gas Mark 4.

Remove the chilled tart base from the fridge and trim off the excess pastry from around the edge. Line the tart base with baking parchment, fill it with baking beans, place on a baking tray and blind bake for 20 minutes in the preheated oven. Remove the beans and parchment, then bake the base for 5 more minutes. When the base is done, reduce the oven temperature to 160°c/140°c fan/Gas Mark 3.

For the filling

While the tart base is baking, fry the bacon until crisp in a pan over a medium heat. Place half the halloumi into the baked tart base then add the raw broccoli, radish, courgette and cherry tomatoes. Chop the crispy bacon into small pieces and scatter them over the filling, then lay the remaining halloumi on top.

In a bowl or jug, mix the eggs and milk together, seasoning well with salt and pepper. Pour the egg mixture into the tart base over the filling. Sprinkle over the dried herbs and garlic. Bake the tart in the oven for 40 minutes or until the centre has set. Allow to cool before eating.

KEFTEDES
(CYPRIOT MEATBALLS)

MAKES 22 | PREPARATION TIME: 15 MINUTES | COOKING TIME: 30 MINUTES (OVEN BAKED) OR 6-7 MINUTES (FRIED)

These meatballs are delicious served with orzo in a tomatoey sauce, or even flattened into a sandwich made with white bread while still hot. They are also a vital part of a meze. They are almost as good when oven baked too.

INGREDIENTS

500g pork mince

1 onion, finely chopped

1 medium potato, peeled and grated

15g fresh parsley, finely chopped

1 egg

1 tbsp olive oil

½ tsp cinnamon

Handful of dried mint

1 slice of bread

Sea salt and black pepper

METHOD

Put the mince, onion, and grated potato into a bowl. Add the parsley, egg, olive oil and cinnamon, then rub the mint between the palms of your hands to crush it into the bowl. Season the mixture with salt and pepper.

Add the bread; I always blitz it into breadcrumbs in the food processor because I use homemade bread, which is harder, but if you're using shop-bought sliced bread, you can just throw it in.

Use your hands to mix and squidge everything together. You should be able to form a ball that stays together. If it's too wet, a little more bread; if it's too dry, add a little more olive oil.

Roll the mixture into balls (roughly a bit smaller than a golf ball). If you are using the oven, preheat it to 220°c/200°c fan/Gas Mark 8 and place the keftedes on a baking tray lined with greaseproof paper. Bake them in the oven for about 30 minutes, turning halfway through the cooking time.

If you are deep frying them, it will take about 6 to 7 minutes. I use olive oil (of course!) and turn them occasionally to get a good colour all over.

MACARONIA DOU FOURNOU
(PASTA BAKE WITH PORK)

SERVES 8-10 | PREPARATION TIME: 40-45 MINUTES | COOKING TIME: 45 MINUTES (OR 1 HOUR FROM CHILLED)

This means 'macaroni of the oven'. This popular dish is seldom the same from one household to the other as we all add our own twists. You can make this a day ahead and refrigerate it, so all you need to do before dinner is pop the dish in the oven.

INGREDIENTS

300g no.2 size long macaroni (you could use any tube-shaped pasta instead)

1kg pork mince

1 tsp ground cinnamon

Small bunch of fresh parsley, finely chopped (approx. 20g)

4 tbsp tomato passata

Sea salt and black pepper

Handful of dried mint

200ml vegetable stock

For the béchamel sauce

2 eggs, beaten

100g flour

1 litre milk

1 stock cube or 1 tsp stock powder

100g halloumi, grated

METHOD

Preheat the oven to 200°c/180°c fan/Gas Mark 6. Cook and drain the pasta.

Brown the pork mince in a large pan over a medium-high heat, then add the cinnamon, parsley, passata, salt and pepper. Crush over the handful of dried mint with your hands. Add the stock, bring to the boil and simmer until the liquid has evaporated.

For the béchamel sauce

Place the eggs, flour, milk and stock cube or powder into the pan and stir it all well together using a whisk. Keep stirring over the heat until the sauce thickens, then stir in most of the halloumi and save the rest.

Before assembling the macaronia dou fournou, add a few spoonfuls of béchamel to the meat sauce and stir in to make it creamy.

To assemble, place half the cooked macaroni into an ovenproof dish. You can line it up perfectly or throw it in; according to my Yiayia, this shows what sort of person you are, but I would say it depends on how busy you are! The next layer is half of the meat sauce, followed by a thin layer of the béchamel sauce, the remaining meat sauce and then finally the remaining béchamel sauce. Sprinkle the grated halloumi over the top and bake in the oven for 45 minutes (or about an hour from chilled) or until the cheese is bubbling and golden.

MEDITERRANEAN PASTA BAKE

SERVES 4 | PREPARATION TIME: 15 MINUTES | COOKING TIME: 1 HOUR

I use my basic Mediterranean vegetables as the base for this recipe. This is a great vegan dish, but you can add halloumi, chorizo, loukanika, tuna, chicken or whatever takes your fancy.

INGREDIENTS

300g pasta (I like rigatoni best, but any will work)

1 courgette

1 aubergine

1 yellow pepper

1 orange pepper

10 baby plum tomatoes

250g mushrooms

Generous drizzle of OliveOlive Oregano Fused Olive Oil

400g tinned chopped tomatoes

10 black olives

10 green olives

60g spinach, roughly chopped

Sea salt and black pepper

METHOD

Preheat the oven to 200°c/180°c fan/Gas Mark 6. Boil the pasta and drain when cooked.

Roughly chop all the vegetables and place them into a deep roasting tray, drizzle over the oil and mix it all together so that the oil coats all the vegetables. Roast for 35 to 40 minutes until the vegetables are nicely caramelised.

Remove the roasted vegetables from the oven and reduce the temperature to 180°c/160°c fan/Gas Mark 4. Add the cooked pasta, chopped tinned tomatoes, olives, and spinach. Mix everything together, season to taste with salt and pepper, then cover the roasting tray with foil. Place in the oven to bake for 15 to 20 minutes.

MEDITERRANEAN VEGETABLES WITH GIANT COUSCOUS

SERVES 4 | PREPARATION TIME: 10 MINUTES | COOKING TIME: 45-55 MINUTES

We really are fans of roasted vegetables in our house.
This is just another way of getting some of your five a day in.

INGREDIENTS

1 courgette

1 aubergine

1 yellow pepper

1 orange pepper

10 baby plum tomatoes

250g mushrooms

Generous drizzle of OliveOlive Chilli Fused Olive Oil

Sea salt and black pepper

1 tsp smoked paprika

200g giant couscous

400ml vegetable stock

METHOD

Preheat the oven to 200˚c/180˚c fan/Gas Mark 6.

Roughly chop all the vegetables and place them into a deep roasting tray. Drizzle over the oil, season with salt and pepper, then stir in the smoked paprika.

Roast the vegetables in the preheated oven for 35 to 40 minutes until they are nicely caramelised.

Take the tray out of the oven, then add the couscous and stock. Cover the tray with foil and return it to the oven for 10 to 15 minutes, or until the couscous is cooked and the stock has been absorbed.

MOROCCAN STYLE CHICKEN

SERVES 4-6 | PREPARATION TIME: 15 MINUTES | COOKING TIME: 1 HOUR

This one-dish meal is easy to make and perfect for the family or casual dining with friends. It's delicious with some Greek yoghurt on the side.

INGREDIENTS

4 carrots

7 potatoes

100g dried apricots

12 chicken thigh fillets

Sea salt and black pepper

Generous drizzle of extra virgin olive oil

½ tsp ground cinnamon

½ tsp sumac

1 tsp cumin seeds, crushed

200g frozen fine green beans

400g tinned chopped tomatoes

400ml vegetable stock

METHOD

Preheat the oven to 220°c/200°c fan/Gas Mark 7.

Peel the carrots then cut them into quarters (halves if they are skinny) to make batons roughly 6cm long. Wash the potatoes then cut them into wedges. Try to keep them all a similar size for more even cooking. Cut the dried apricots into little pieces, or you can buy them already chopped.

Place the chicken into a large roasting tray, season it with salt and pepper, add a generous drizzle of olive oil and then add all the other ingredients to the tray.

Mix everything together well and place into the preheated oven, uncovered, to cook for 20 minutes. Remove from the oven, stir everything again and cover the tray with foil, then return it to the oven for a further 30 minutes. Take out the tray, remove the foil, stir the mixture again and return to the oven, uncovered, for a final 10 minute blast before serving.

PATATES ME T'AVYA
(CYPRIOT STYLE FRIED POTATOES WITH EGGS)

SERVES 4 | PREPARATION TIME: 20 MINUTES | COOKING TIME: 30 MINUTES

This means 'potatoes with eggs' but it is so much more than that. As with many of my dishes, I don't have an actual recipe for this because I just add whatever I have in the fridge or cupboard, so this is my favourite combination of ingredients.

INGREDIENTS

6-8 medium-sized potatoes

350ml extra virgin olive oil (for deep frying)

250g mushrooms

1 medium-sized courgette

½ a chorizo sausage

280g jarred artichoke hearts

125g halloumi, diced

3-4 large spinach leaves

4-5 eggs

Sea salt and black pepper

METHOD

Peel the potatoes and cut them into similar-sized cubes. Heat the olive oil in a large pan and deep fry the potatoes until they are golden. Remove them from the pan and place in a bowl lined with kitchen roll to mop up the excess oil.

Chop the mushrooms and courgettes into small pieces. Place a little of the hot oil from the potatoes into a large, shallow frying pan. Add the mushrooms and courgettes to this pan and fry until they are soft.

Halve the chorizo lengthways, then slice and add it to the pan. Stir in until the chorizo is cooked. Chop the artichoke hearts and throw them in, followed by the diced halloumi. Stir well. Cut the spinach leaves in half down the centre spine and then slice up. Add the spinach to the pan and stir until it has wilted.

Stir in the fried potatoes, keeping the heat high, then break the eggs into the pan. Stir well until the eggs are cooked, season to taste, and serve.

CHLOE GEORGIADES

RAVIOLES

SERVES 4 AS A MAIN (MAKES 60) | PREPARATION TIME: 1-1½ HOURS, PLUS 30 MINUTES RESTING | COOKING TIME: 8 MINUTES

Cypriot ravioles are filled with halloumi and mint. This is my mum's recipe. You can buy these frozen in Cyprus, and in Greek groceries in the larger UK cities, but as I'm in Cambridgeshire I have learnt to make my own. It's not as hard as you think!

INGREDIENTS

For the pasta

500g plain flour

2 tbsp olive oil

Pinch of salt

200ml lukewarm water

For the filling

375g halloumi, plus extra to garnish

2 medium eggs

Generous handful of dried mint, crushed

Stock cube or 1 tsp stock powder (optional)

METHOD

For the pasta

Put the flour, olive oil and salt into a bowl. Slowly add the water and stir to form a dough. Cover and leave to rest for a minimum of 30 minutes, and up to 1 hour.

For the filling

Grate all the halloumi and put the 375g in a bowl with the eggs and mint. The mixture should be firm; if it's too wet add more halloumi, or more olive oil if it's too dry.

Roll the chilled dough into thin sheets. A pasta machine provides approximately 15cm wide strips so if you are using a rolling pin, cut your sheets into 15cm strips.

Mould the halloumi mix with a teaspoon and place the blobs every 2cm along the rolled-out dough towards the top, leaving a 1cm border above. Fold the dough over so that the filling is on the bottom, closed edge. Using the top half of a cookie cutter, cut out the ravioles into semi-circles, ensuring the halloumi mix is sealed inside.

Bring a large pan of water almost to the boil. If you're adding stock to the water, go easy because halloumi is quite salty. Add the ravioles to the pan and slightly lower the heat. Cook for approximately 8 minutes, using a slotted spoon to push them down from time to time, but avoid stirring. Lift out with the slotted spoon and serve straight away with some grated halloumi on top.

ROLLO
(MEATBALLS IN TOMATO SAUCE)

SERVES 4 | PREPARATION TIME: 15 MINUTES | COOKING TIME: 35-40 MINUTES

Rollo is usually one big ball of meat, a bit like meatloaf, but I like to make smaller meatballs which go beautifully with pasta, orzo, or potatoes. If you're having it with pasta or orzo you must finish it off with some grated halloumi!

INGREDIENTS

500g minced pork

1 onion, finely chopped

1 tsp ground cinnamon

20g fresh parsley, finely chopped

2 eggs, separated

Sea salt and black pepper

100g breadcrumbs

5 tbsp extra virgin olive oil

150ml red wine

400g tinned chopped tomatoes

METHOD

In a large bowl, combine the minced pork with the onion, cinnamon, parsley, egg yolks, salt and pepper. Use your hands to mix everything together and add some of the breadcrumbs until the mixture stays together when moulded into a ball.

Roll the mixture into eight balls using your hands, then coat each one first in the egg whites and then in the remaining breadcrumbs. Place the prepared rollo on a plate.

Heat the olive oil in a deep, heavy-based pan. It should just about cover the base of the pan. Add the meatballs to the hot oil and shallow fry. Do not be tempted to turn the meatballs too soon, as you might break them. Gently tease the meatball away from the base of the pan, and if it comes away easily they are ready to turn. Continue to fry until they are browned all over.

Add the wine and tomatoes to the browned meatballs, stir well, lower the heat, cover the pan and simmer for 20 minutes before serving.

SOUVLAKI
(GREEK STYLE KEBAB)

SERVES 6 | PREPARATION TIME: 10 MINUTES, PLUS MARINATING IF DESIRED | COOKING TIME: 30 MINUTES

Souvlaki means 'little souvla' which are bigger pieces of meat cooked on a barbecue rotisserie. If you don't have a rotisserie, you can use skewers. You can also cook souvlaki under the grill on skewers, and you can substitute lamb or chicken for the pork.

INGREDIENTS

1kg pork shoulder, cut into 2.5cm cubes

3 tbsp extra virgin olive oil

1 lemon, juiced

Sea salt and black pepper

Good pinch of dried oregano

METHOD

Put the diced pork into a bowl, pour in the oil and lemon juice then add salt and pepper. Mix well so that the oil completely coats the meat. Cover and refrigerate until you are ready to cook it. You can prepare your meat ahead of time, leaving it to marinade for a few hours or overnight for optimum flavour.

If you are using wooden skewers, soak them in water before use to prevent them from burning on the ends. Thread the cubes of meat onto the skewers and cook on a hot barbecue or under the grill, turning frequently if not using a rotisserie.

Once the meat is seared on all sides, add pinches of oregano as it turns or occasionally when you turn it. Cook for approximately 30 minutes or until the meat is done. Serve with Cyprus chips and salad or in a pitta bread with salad.

STUFF THAT! CHICKEN

SERVES 4 | PREPARATION TIME: 25 MINUTES | COOKING TIME: 1 HOUR

This is a family favourite, and one that looks more complicated than it is to make. The combination of flavours from the bacon and the halloumi complement the chicken perfectly.

INGREDIENTS

1 red pepper, roughly chopped

1 yellow pepper, roughly chopped

1 courgette, thinly sliced

1 red onion, thinly sliced

1 leek, chopped into chunky discs

20 cherry tomatoes

2 cloves of garlic, grated or crushed

Generous drizzle of OliveOlive Garlic Fused Olive Oil

Sea salt and black pepper

½ a block of halloumi

8 boneless, skinless chicken thighs

16 rashers of smoked streaky bacon

Easy Pesto Dressing (see page 38)

METHOD

Preheat the oven to 220°c/200°c fan/Gas Mark 7.

Place all the prepared vegetables into a roasting tray. Stir in the grated or crushed garlic, drizzle everything with the garlic olive oil and season with salt and pepper (but don't go overboard with the salt as there is plenty in the bacon and halloumi).

Slice the halloumi into long thick chunks and place them inside the fold of the chicken thighs. Roll them up and wrap with bacon, using two slices per thigh. Place the wrapped chicken thighs on the bed of vegetables and cover the whole tray with foil.

Place the tray in the preheated oven to cook the chicken and vegetables for 45 minutes. Check and stir the mixture every 15 minutes. After 45 minutes, remove the foil and roast uncovered for a further 15 minutes. Drizzle with some of the Easy Pesto Dressing to serve.

TAVA
(SLOW COOKED LAMB & POTATOES)

SERVES 4-6 | PREPARATION TIME: 15 MINUTES | COOKING TIME: 2 HOURS

This traditional Cypriot one dish meal is typically made with lamb, but you can also use pork or chicken. Cooking everything slowly in one dish means that all the flavours combine. It's easy to make and tasty: a total win-win!

INGREDIENTS

1kg lamb (I use neck fillets, but chops work too)

7 medium-sized potatoes

1 tsp cumin seeds

3 bay leaves

Sea salt and black pepper

60ml olive oil

4-5 tomatoes, quartered

100ml white wine

100ml water

METHOD

Preheat the oven to 180°c/160°c fan/Gas Mark 5.

Place the meat into a large roasting tray. Peel and cut the potatoes into large thick discs then add them to the tray around the lamb.

Crush the cumin seeds using a pestle and mortar then sprinkle them into the tray with the bay leaves. Season with salt and pepper, then pour in the olive oil and mix well so that it coats everything.

Throw over the quartered tomatoes and add the wine and the water; take care not to rinse the ingredients with the liquids, but pour them into a gap so they fill the bottom of the tray.

Cover the dish with foil and put it in the preheated oven for 2 hours. You can check on it and turn the meat after an hour, but this isn't essential.

Serve with a green salad and some Greek yoghurt.

THAT CHICKEN AND OLIVE THING

SERVES 4-6 | PREPARATION TIME: 15 MINUTES | COOKING TIME: 1 HOUR

I made this recipe up quite a few years ago and we didn't have a name for it, so we just called it 'that chicken and olive thing'. I have adapted it over the years to make it even easier, so this is my most up-to-date version.

INGREDIENTS

8 boneless, skinless chicken thigh fillets (approximately 1kg)

12 rashers of smoked back bacon, roughly chopped (approximately 300g)

3 cloves of garlic, crushed

1 tbsp dried oregano

Black pepper

Generous drizzle of extra virgin olive oil

1 large leek, sliced

1 yellow or orange pepper, roughly chopped

2 red peppers, roughly chopped

250g pitted olives (I like to have a mixture of green and black)

150ml white wine

150g halloumi, diced

METHOD

Preheat the oven to 200°c/180°c fan/Gas Mark 6.

Place the chicken pieces, bacon, garlic, oregano, black pepper and olive oil into a deep ovenproof dish. Mix everything well and place uncovered into the centre of the preheated oven to cook for 20 minutes.

Remove the dish from the oven and add the leek, peppers, olives and wine. Stir well, making sure that all the chicken pieces have been turned over, and return to the oven for 35 more minutes, stirring halfway through the cooking time and turning the chicken pieces over again.

Remove the dish from the oven, turn the chicken pieces once more, then add the diced halloumi. Return the dish to the oven for a final 5 minutes before serving.

TUNA ROSEMARY SKEWERS

SERVES 2 | PREPARATION TIME: 15 MINUTES, PLUS UP TO 1 HOUR MARINATING | COOKING TIME: 4-6 MINUTES

Frank says: "I'm a private chef and met Rob and Pam at a food festival; OliveOlive have supplied me with their delicious extra virgin olive oil ever since. This combination of tuna in a simple oil-based marinade, serrano ham and rosemary from my own herb garden is perfect on a summer's day, washed down with a crisp white wine."

INGREDIENTS

4 sprigs of rosemary

2 cloves of garlic

Good splash of olive oil

½ a lemon, juiced

Black pepper

2 best quality tuna steaks

6 slices of serrano ham or Parma ham

METHOD

Strip most of the rosemary leaves from the stalks, leaving a few leaves on at the tip. Finely chop the stripped leaves, crush or finely chop the garlic, then combine the rosemary and garlic with the oil, lemon juice and black pepper to make a marinade.

Cut each tuna steak into six evenly sized pieces, toss them in the rosemary and garlic mixture, then leave to marinate for at least 10 minutes and up to 1 hour, chilled.

Cut each piece of serrano or Parma ham lengthways to make thin strips. Wrap each piece of marinated tuna in a strip of ham.

Use a wooden or metal skewer to make a hole through the centre of a piece of wrapped tuna, then push it onto a rosemary stalk. Repeat until you have threaded three pieces of wrapped tuna onto each rosemary stalk.

Lightly oil a griddle pan (or use the barbecue) and heat it up. Griddle the tuna skewers for 2 to 3 minutes on each side.

Serve with salads, or as an appetiser. This recipe also works well with monkfish, or you could try it with halloumi!

SWEET &
SAVOURY TREATS

BANANA BREAD

MAKES 1 X 2LB LOAF | PREPARATION TIME: 10-15 MINUTES | COOKING TIME: 45 MINUTES

This is a gluten-free banana bread from our friend Anita, using our olive oil. You can of course use normal self-raising flour instead of gluten-free, and if you're not keen on pumpkin seeds you can sprinkle over some Demerara sugar instead before putting the loaf into the oven.

INGREDIENTS

4 ripe bananas

125ml olive oil

185g soft brown sugar

2 eggs

1 tsp vanilla extract

1 tsp ground cinnamon

2 tbsp warm milk

1 tsp bicarbonate of soda

1 tsp baking powder

270g gluten-free self-raising flour

Pumpkin seeds (optional)

1 banana, sliced (optional)

Demerara and icing sugar

METHOD

Preheat the oven to 180°c/160°c fan/Gas Mark 4. Lightly oil and flour your loaf tin, or line it with greaseproof paper.

Place the bananas, olive oil, sugar, eggs, vanilla and cinnamon in a food processor, then blitz until smooth. In a small saucepan, heat the milk then whisk in the bicarbonate of soda until it dissolves. Add the baking powder and flour to the food processor, mix them into the batter, then gradually pour in the warm milk while the food processor is running.

Once the mixture is combined, pour into the prepared loaf tin and sprinkle with your choice of pumpkin seeds, sliced banana and Demerara sugar. Bake the banana bread in the preheated oven for 45 minutes or until a skewer comes out clean.

Remove from the oven and leave in the tin to cool before turning out onto a cake plate. Dust with icing sugar to serve. The banana bread keeps well in an airtight tin for up to 4 days.

EASY ELIOPITTES
(OLIVE SCONES)

MAKES ABOUT 24 SCONES | PREPARATION TIME: 15-20 MINUTES | COOKING TIME: 20 MINUTES

This recipe is very special to me as it was my late aunt's recipe and one of the first that I baked as a young girl. You can change it about a bit by using green olives instead of black, or rosemary and oregano instead of mint.

INGREDIENTS

1kg self-raising flour

2 tsp baking powder

250ml extra virgin olive oil

500ml orange juice

500g pitted black olives

1 onion, finely chopped

Handful of dried mint

METHOD

Preheat the oven to 220°c/200°c fan/Gas Mark 7 and brush two muffin trays with olive oil.

In a large bowl, combine the flour, baking powder, olive oil and orange juice.

In a separate bowl, mix together the olives, onion and mint. Add this to the dough, making sure that the olives are evenly distributed.

Add a loaded tablespoon of the olive dough to each hole in the oiled muffin trays, then bake in the preheated oven for approximately 20 minutes.

ZOIRO STEFANI

HALLOUMOPITA

(HALLOUMI PIE)

SERVES 10-12 | PREPARATION TIME: 1 HOUR | COOKING TIME: 40 MINUTES

This recipe calls for mehlepi (an aromatic spice) and mastiha (mastic gum) which are used widely in Cyprus and the Middle East. If you can't get hold of these ingredients, you can just leave them out.

INGREDIENTS

For the pastry

1kg plain flour, plus extra for dusting

1 tsp sugar

1 tsp fine salt

1 tsp baking powder

1 tsp bicarbonate of soda

1¼ tsp (or a 7g sachet) instant yeast

500ml orange juice

250ml extra virgin olive oil

For the filling

1kg halloumi

20g dried mint

¼ tsp mehlepi

¼ tsp mastiha

¼ tsp ground nutmeg

4 eggs

METHOD

For the pastry

Combine all the dry ingredients in a bowl. Pour in the orange juice and olive oil then gently bring the mixture together with your hands until it forms a dough. Leave the pastry to rest in the fridge for 30 minutes. Meanwhile, preheat the oven to 200°c/180°c fan/Gas Mark 6 and make the filling.

For the filling

Grate the halloumi into a bowl. Add the dry ingredients, stirring to coat the halloumi in the herbs and spices, then crack the eggs into the bowl one by one, stirring well each time.

Grease a 30cm round cake tin with olive oil. Divide the pastry into quarters, and roll out one of the pieces into a circular shape that will just overfill the base of the cake tin. Pour over a third of the halloumi filling and level it out. Don't worry if it doesn't reach the sides of the tin.

Roll out another piece of pastry to roughly the same size, lay it into the tin, add another third of filling, and then repeat this process once more. Roll out the last piece of pastry and place it on top of the pie to enclose the filling.

Place an upturned glass into the centre of the pie, then use a sharp knife to cut the pie into 12 to 14 equal segments from the glass to the edge of the tin. Using your hands, twist each segment so the bottom layer comes to the top. Don't worry about the filling spilling out.

Remove the glass and decorate the central circle to your liking. You can use a fork to make tiny dots resembling the centre of a flower, or make leaves out of any leftover dough. Place the pie in the centre of the preheated oven to bake for 40 minutes or until golden.

CHLOE GEORGIADES

KATIMERIA
(CINNAMON PASTRIES)

MAKES 18-20 | PREPARATION TIME: 30 MINUTES, PLUS 30 MINUTES RESTING TIME | COOKING TIME: 15-20 MINUTES

My mum's cinnamon pastries are lovely with a Greek coffee or a cup of English tea. I trialled this at home because my mum's recipe said 'a glass of oil.' When I asked more about the glass, she said: 'the one we drink water from!'

INGREDIENTS

For the pastry

500g self-raising flour

Pinch of fine salt

1 tsp baking powder

125g extra virgin olive oil

150ml lukewarm water

For the filling

100g roughly ground almonds

2 tsp ground cinnamon

50g caster sugar, plus extra for dusting

50ml extra virgin olive oil

METHOD

For the pastry

Add the flour, salt, and baking powder to a bowl. Pour in the olive oil, then gradually add the water while using your hands to bring everything together until the mixture forms a dough. You may not need all the water, or you may need a little more. Leave the pastry to rest for 30 minutes.

For the filling

Mix the almonds, cinnamon, and sugar together in a bowl. Pour the olive oil into a small cup (my mum says a Greek coffee cup will do!) and set aside. Preheat the oven to 200°c/180°c fan/Gas Mark 6.

Shape the pastry into a large tube and cut into 9 or 10 slices. Roll each slice out into thin rectangular sheets about 35 by 15cm, then cut each sheet into two smaller rectangles; this will make two katimeria. You should have 18 to 20 sheets in total.

Take a sheet, brush it with olive oil and sprinkle some of the almond and cinnamon filling over the whole rectangle using a teaspoon. Roll up the pastry from the bottom to the top so you have a tube, then roll the tube into a spiral. Repeat this process with all the pastry sheets.

Place the pastries on a baking tray lined with greaseproof paper and bake in the preheated oven for 15 to 20 minutes until golden. Remove them from the oven and leave to cool on a wire tray. Sprinkle the pastries with a little caster sugar before serving.

MAMMA'S TRADITIONAL ELIOPITTES
(MINI OLIVE PASTRIES)

MAKES 28 | PREPARATION TIME: 1 HOUR, PLUS 1 HOUR RESTING | COOKING TIME: 25 MINUTES

Whenever we stay with my parents, there is always an endless supply of these. My mum wakes up early and gets her baking out of the way, especially in the summer when it is too hot to bake in the heat of the day.

INGREDIENTS

For the pastry

500g plain flour

½ tsp salt

125ml extra virgin olive oil

125ml orange juice

4 tbsp lukewarm water

For the filling and topping

100g sesame seeds

200g pitted black olives

1 onion, finely chopped

Handful of dried mint

METHOD

For the pastry

Place the flour, salt and olive oil into a bowl and combine them with your hands. Add the orange juice and continue to mix with your hands. Add the water a tablespoon at a time until the mixture forms a dough. Leave the dough to rest for a minimum of 30 minutes.

For the filling and topping

Soak then drain the sesame seeds, and lay them out to dry on a clean tea towel. In a bowl, mix the olives with the onion and mint. Preheat the oven to 200°c/180°c fan/Gas Mark 6. Pour the prepared sesame seeds into a shallow bowl.

Roll the chilled pastry into thin sheets and cut into approximately 5.5 by 4cm rectangles. Place a rectangle into the sesame seeds to coat the outside and place a spoonful of filling in the centre. Roll into a tube and secure the ends. Place with the seal end down onto a baking sheet lined with baking parchment. Repeat this each time to make as many pastries as the dough or filling allows. Cut the ends off if they are too long and reuse the pastry, so it goes a bit further and don't worry if there are extra sesame seeds on it!

Bake the pastries in the oven for 25 minutes, or until golden. The eliopittes can be frozen so it's worth making a double batch.

ORANGE, DARK CHOCOLATE AND OLIVE OIL CAKE

SERVES 12 | PREPARATION TIME: 30 MINUTES | COOKING TIME: 40-45 MINUTES IN A CAKE TIN
OR 30-35 MINUTES IN MUFFIN TINS

Lindsey says: "I first came across this cake on a trip to Spain. It was so good we had to recreate it on my return! Of course, we only use OliveOlive's extra virgin olive oil as it works so beautifully here. This cake looks lovely when baked in a Bundt tin but a regular 23cm round cake tin or muffin tins will also work, just note the different cooking times.

INGREDIENTS

Knob of butter, melted

300g golden caster sugar

5 large eggs

3 oranges, zested and juiced
(approximately 150ml of juice)

150ml olive oil

280g self-raising flour, sieved

60g dark chocolate chips

METHOD

Preheat the oven to 160°c/140°c fan/Gas Mark 4. Grease your tin well with the melted butter.

Put the sugar, eggs and orange zest in a bowl and whisk with an electric mixer on full speed until thick and pale for approximately 5 minutes. With the mixer running on a medium to low speed, drizzle in the orange juice and olive oil until fully combined.

Add the sieved flour to the bowl and whisk until you have a smooth batter. Stir in the chocolate chips. Pour the mixture into your prepared tin and bake in the oven for 40 to 45 minutes or until a skewer inserted into the cake comes out clean.

Allow the cake to cool for 10 minutes before turning out onto a wire rack to cool completely. It will keep in an airtight container for 3 to 4 days, and can be frozen for up to 3 months.

YIAYIA'S APPLE CAKE

SERVES 10-12 | PREPARATION TIME: 15 MINUTES | COOKING TIME: 40 MINUTES

My Yiayia (grandmother) lived with us when I was little. I spent lots of time with her in the kitchen, learning many traditional Cypriot recipes. This one is quite special to me as it brings back lots of memories of her.

INGREDIENTS

400g apples

2 tbsp sugar

2 tsp ground cinnamon

125ml olive oil

100g caster sugar

125ml milk

2 eggs

280g self-raising flour

1 tsp baking powder

Demerara sugar (optional)

METHOD

Preheat the oven to 180°c/160°c fan/Gas Mark 4. Peel the apples then chop them into small cubes. Place into a bowl and sprinkle over the sugar and cinnamon. Mix well and leave to one side while you make the cake batter.

In another bowl, mix the olive oil and caster sugar together. Add the milk and eggs, stir well with a wooden spoon, then gradually add the flour, mixing it in a little at a time. Lastly, add the baking powder. Mix the batter well to make sure there are no lumpy bits.

Tip the apples into the cake batter and stir well. Pour into a 22cm round cake tin, smooth out the surface and add a generous sprinkling of Demerara sugar. This gives the top a lovely sweet crunch because the cake itself is not overly sweet.

Bake the cake in the preheated oven for 40 minutes. Check whether it's ready by inserting a skewer into the centre; if the skewer comes out clean it's done. If there's some mixture clinging to the skewer, leave the cake in the oven for a few more minutes then check again.

Leave to cool slightly in the tin before turning out and cooling completely.